Original title:
Quieted Wisps Above the Phoenix Drain

Author: Aron Pilviste
ISBN HARDBACK: 978-1-80562-765-4
ISBN PAPERBACK: 978-1-80564-286-2

The Tranquil Flame's Return

In stillness, whispers weave the night,
A flicker stirs, sparks take flight.
Soft embers dance in secret way,
As dreams awaken, where shadows play.

Beneath the stars, a promise glows,
Of hidden paths, where magic flows.
Each heart recalls the ember's song,
Resilient warmth, where souls belong.

Once lost in depths of darkest shade,
The tranquil flame, now unafraid.
It calls to hearts, a guiding light,
Illuminating hopes in flight.

With every flicker, peace unfurls,
A tapestry of hidden worlds.
Where courage blooms in gentle sway,
And truth emerges from dismay.

So let us gather, hand in hand,
Around the fire, on golden sand.
For in this glow, our spirits rise,
To greet the dawn, 'neath open skies.

Veils of Radiance and Shadows

In twilight's hush, the mists descend,
Where light and dark entwine, they blend.
Veils of radiance, soft and bright,
Guard secrets held in fleeting flight.

Whispers linger 'neath the moon,
Echoes of a timeless tune.
Shadows stretch with silent grace,
In this enchanted, hidden space.

Glistening dreams in silver thread,
Weave stories of the lost and dead.
Each shimmer holds a tale untold,
Of bravery and hearts of gold.

Yet in the shade, a flicker gleams,
A glimmer born from fervent dreams.
For in the dark, there lies a spark,
That guides the weary through the dark.

As dawn unfolds, the veils will part,
Revealing treasures that fill the heart.
For only through the darkness roam,
Can one unveil their truest home.

Silhouettes of the Searing Past

In shadows deep, where secrets play,
Whispers linger, night and day.
Fragments of dreams, lost in the mist,
Echoes of souls that once existed.

Time’s cruel hand, it drags us near,
To memories carved in crystal clear.
Flickering lights of bygone grace,
Reminders of our fleeting place.

Each choice made, a step in woe,
Paths diverged, but where to go?
Serpents of fate, with tongues of fire,
Breathe life into our heart's desire.

Yet hope remains, a fragile thread,
Ties to the living, ties to the dead.
In the tapestry, we find the core,
Of love and loss, forevermore.

So let us dance in the starlit glow,
Embrace the past that we once sowed.
For in the silhouettes, we see the light,
Guiding us home through the endless night.

Woven Threads of Air and Fire

Threads of silver spun with gold,
Dancing softly, stories told.
Whispers of winds that twine and curl,
Weave the fabric of every world.

Flames igniting, the spirit’s flare,
Embers flicker in the midnight air.
Hearts entwined in a radiant thread,
Binding the living to those long dead.

Each moment stitched with tender care,
A tapestry rich, a breath, a prayer.
In every spark, a magic spark,
Illuminates the profound and stark.

So let the winds of change arise,
Scattering dreams across the skies.
In the brilliance of air and fire,
Lies the soul's immutable desire.

Together they dance, entwined as one,
Under the moon, beneath the sun.
For in every thread, a story glows,
A legacy born as time bestows.

Lullabies for the Fallen

Softly sung, the lullabies flow,
Echoes of dreams in twilight's glow.
For those who walked on paths unknown,
In the hush of night, they find their home.

Gentle whispers through the trees,
Carrying hopes upon the breeze.
A melody played for hearts now still,
Binding their spirits with love's sweet will.

Each note a memory, tenderly spun,
Celebrating the lives of many, not one.
With every heartbeat, they softly stir,
Remnants of laughter, a wistful blur.

And as we lay them down to rest,
We hold their stories to our chest.
The echoes linger, never far,
Guiding us softly like a star.

So let us sing those lullabies clear,
For every spirit, held so dear.
In these sweet chords, they shall remain,
Forever part of our joyful refrain.

Rise of the Gentle Incandescence

In the dawn where shadows wane,
A light emerges, free from pain.
The gentle incandescence blooms,
Chasing away the deepest glooms.

With every breath, a spark ignites,
Filling the world with vibrant lights.
A flicker here, a shimmer there,
Stirring souls to awaken, aware.

Through silken threads of twilight's hue,
The promise of hope begins anew.
In quiet corners, dreams take flight,
Illuminating the longest night.

So rise, ye hearts, with purpose strong,
Join in the chorus, the ancient song.
For in the glow of love's embrace,
We find our way, we find our place.

As golden rays dissolve the dark,
Within us all ignites a spark.
Together we shall dare to be,
The gentle incandescence, wild and free.

Veils of Calm over Radiant Winds

A gentle breeze in twilight's fold,
Whispers of secrets yet untold.
The stars awaken, soft and bright,
Painting the sky with threads of light.

Through golden fields where shadows play,
Nature’s song ignites the day.
The silence hums a soothing tune,
As dawn begins to greet the moon.

Each leaf a dancer in the air,
Twirling dreams without a care.
In every flutter, peace bestows,
A realm where endless wonder grows.

With every gust, fresh tales are spun,
Creating magic 'neath the sun.
Veils of calm in rhythmic sway,
Guide us through this tranquil gray.

So let the radiant winds embrace,
Our hearts entwined in nature’s grace.
For in this moment, pure and fair,
We find our solace, free from despair.

Sighs of Light in the Ember's Wake

As shadows dance in embers' glow,
Sighs of light begin to flow.
Each flicker tells of days gone past,
Whispers linger, shadows cast.

In twilight whispers, secrets share,
A fragile glow, a tender flare.
Heartbeats echo, soft and slow,
Carried gently by winds that know.

The stars above begin to rise,
Glimmers of hope in obsidian skies.
Each spark a promise, shining bright,
Drawing forth dreams from the night.

In the ember's warm embrace,
Time stands still, a fleeting space.
Tender sighs of warmth invite,
A cozy realm where hearts ignite.

From the ashes, stories bloom,
Light emerges, dispelling gloom.
Together in this glowing fate,
We find our way, we illuminate.

Echoing Whispers of the Rebirth

Within the hush of dawn’s sweet breath,
Echoes linger, dispelling death.
With every note that fills the air,
Life unfurls from slumber’s lair.

The budding flowers start to rise,
Painting the earth with vibrant sighs.
Sheltered dreams take flight anew,
In the morn's embrace, each heart rings true.

Through dew-kissed leaves and radiant beams,
Nature hums her ancient dreams.
Awakening souls, both shy and bold,
Tales of rebirth gently told.

With every heartbeat, whispers swell,
Binding worlds in a silent spell.
A dance of life, so pure, so bright,
Echoing through the endless night.

For in these moments, hope is found,
As the cosmos spins round and round.
Embracing change with open hearts,
We cherish the magic that never departs.

Solitude Beneath the Flame's Embrace

In silence deep, where shadows dwell,
Solitude weaves her whispered spell.
Beneath the flame's warm, watchful gaze,
Time unfolds in a soft, sweet haze.

The flickering light leads thoughts astray,
While stars above begin to play.
In the stillness, dreams ignite,
Luminous visions take their flight.

Cloaked in night's serene embrace,
We find our truth, our destined place.
Each solitary heartbeat sings,
Of worlds unseen and ancient things.

Through every sigh and every tear,
Solitude brings the heart so near.
Beneath the flame, we fiercely rise,
Embracing life with open eyes.

In the quiet, we connect,
With hidden wonders, bark's effect.
As shadows dance, our spirits soar,
In solitude, we learn to explore.

Cherished Echoes in the Void

In shadows where the whispers dwell,
Memories flicker, a muted bell.
Voices drift on winds of time,
A haunting song, a gentle rhyme.

Stars above in silent gaze,
Guide the heart through endless maze.
Their light a thread in dark's embrace,
Holding tight, a warm, soft place.

Moments lost but never far,
Each heartbeat shines like a rare star.
In forgotten realms, they softly glow,
Cherished echoes of what we know.

In chambers deep, where secrets lay,
Time weaves dreams that gently play.
A symphony of ghosts we hear,
In the void, we hold them near.

From dusk to dawn, they softly call,
A tapestry where shadows fall.
In the silence, love finds its voice,
In whispers, we are given choice.

Chasing the Dimming Light

Beneath the sky, where shadows creep,
A distant glow begins to seep.
In twilight's grasp, we seek the flame,
Calling forth the night's sweet name.

The path ahead, a winding tale,
Guided by stars, we cannot fail.
Though shadows stretch, and fears may rise,
Hope ignites in the darkened skies.

With every step, the echoes fade,
Flickering dreams in the moonlight played.
A dance of shadows, a playful chase,
In the dimming light, we find our place.

The heart beats on, a steady drum,
In the quiet night, we will succumb.
To the calls of night, we answer clear,
Chasing warmth, we draw it near.

As dusk gives way to the deep of night,
We draw upon our inner light.
With courage found, we push through fright,
And dance together in the fading light.

Sighs Amidst the Serene

In gardens lush, where silence reigns,
A gentle breeze, a soft refrain.
Petals fall like whispered dreams,
Sighs float by in tender streams.

The world hushed down, as time doth pause,
In every moment, life gives cause.
Each leaf a story, softly penned,
Where beginnings blend with gentle end.

The stars above in perfect peace,
We find in stillness, sweet release.
With every sigh, a burden shed,
In tranquil moments, spirits fed.

Reflections deep in waters clear,
Show us treasures that draw us near.
In the calm, we breathe anew,
Sighs amidst the serene, so true.

Through evening's haze, our worries cease,
In the embrace of quiet peace.
In nature's arms, we softly lean,
Finding solace in the serene.

Remnants of a Flame's Caress

In embers' glow, where memories dance,
Flickering shadows in a fleeting trance.
Each warmth a whisper, a fleeting breath,
Remnants linger beyond our death.

The crackling fires, they softly sing,
Echoes of joy that the night can bring.
In every spark, a story shared,
A tapestry of love declared.

With every flicker, a story unfolds,
Of hearts entwined and secrets told.
In the dying light, we find our grace,
Remnants of a flame's soft caress.

As shadows lengthen, we hold on tight,
To the flickering hopes that pierce the night.
For in each ember lies a spark,
Guiding our paths through the chilly dark.

Through whispered flames, we find our way,
In the fading glow, we choose to stay.
For the remnants left, they softly bless,
The warmth we carry from love's caress.

Halos in the Hushed Night

In shadows deep, the world does sleep,
Stars twinkle soft, their secrets keep.
The moonlight whispers through the trees,
A gentle hum carried by the breeze.

Night's embrace, a cloak of dreams,
Where magic dances and twilight gleams.
The echo of wishes, a haunting song,
In the held breath of the night, we belong.

Softly the halos begin to glow,
In the silence, forgotten dreams flow.
Ephemeral sparks in the velvet dark,
Illuminating paths, igniting the spark.

Ghosts of daylight fade from sight,
Wrapped in the warmth of the starry light.
With every glance at the sky so bright,
We find our hearts take flight through the night.

So linger here, in this tranquil space,
Let the quiet magic slowly embrace.
For in this hush, we come alive,
In the halos of night, our dreams will thrive.

Flickers of Time in the Void

In the quiet, whispers thread,
Each moment’s light, a tale unsaid.
Flickers of time, a dance divine,
In the endless void, the stars align.

Fragments of yesterday swirl and weave,
In shadows lingering, we believe.
Memory's flicker, a beacon bright,
Guiding the lost through the endless night.

Embers of time, they rise and fall,
A heartbeat’s echo, a distant call.
With every flicker, a choice is made,
In the tapestry of life, we find our way.

With every breath, a story lives,
In the space between, the heart forgives.
In the void's embrace, we shall explore,
The mysteries hidden behind every door.

So gather your dreams, let them take flight,
In the flickers of time, all things feel right.
For within the silence, we learn to see,
The beauty of moments, just you and me.

Endings That Spark New Beginnings

As autumn leaves drift from the trees,
Whispers of change float on the breeze.
Each ending painted in hues of grace,
A canvas where dreams find their place.

In twilight's glow, the past concedes,
A gentle reminder that life proceeds.
For every close, a door swings wide,
In the embrace of change, we must abide.

When shadows fall and silence reigns,
The heart's resilience through joys and pains.
In every sunset, a dawn will rise,
A promise gleaming in the morning skies.

So hold on tight as the seasons shift,
For every ending is a precious gift.
In the tapestry of time, we find our thread,
Weaving the tales of all that’s said.

Embrace the new with courage strong,
For in each ending, we all belong.
With every heartbeat, life sings its tune,
From endings that spark, we’ll chase our moons.

Glistening in the Wake of Fire

In the twilight's glow, embers dance,
Casting shadows in a fleeting trance.
Reflections glimmer, the night does inspire,
Stories are born in the wake of fire.

The warmth it draws, like a gentle sigh,
Whispers of flames that reach for the sky.
Each flicker a promise, a hope untold,
In the heart of darkness, a future bold.

Ashes of yesterday scattered wide,
In their remnants, we learn to abide.
For from the fire, new life shall sprout,
A phoenix of dreams, casting doubt out.

So gather around, let your spirit ignite,
In the glow of the fire that warms the night.
Glistening whispers in warm embrace,
Reminding us all of our sacred place.

With every spark, let our dreams take flight,
In the wake of fire, we find our light.
For in this warmth, we are never alone,
In the heart of the fire, our journey is sown.

The Calm Following Fire's Fury

In the silence after flames,
Whispers of hope softly reign.
The earth, once scorched and bare,
Breathes new life in gentle air.

Ashen remnants start to heal,
The heart learns now to feel.
From embers rise the dreams anew,
A promise held in morning dew.

Sky painted in hues of gold,
Stories of survival told.
Time weaves its tender thread,
Binding all that once lay dead.

Nature hums a soothing song,
Where the brave have felt so wrong.
In the calm, the spirits soar,
Finding peace forevermore.

Let us walk this path with care,
Grateful hearts, our souls laid bare.
In the aftermath of strife,
We cherish all that brings us life.

Tranquility Above the Flickering Night

Above the world so dark and vast,
Stars shimmer like a dream unsurpassed.
The moon, a guardian, glows so bright,
Casting shadows in the quiet night.

A breeze whispers soft lullabies,
The rustle of leaves, the night birds' cries.
In this realm where secrets weave,
Warmth in the darkness we believe.

Glances exchanged with the celestial,
Moments that feel almost ethereal.
Safe in the hush, let worries drift,
In the night's embrace, we softly lift.

With each twinkle, a tale takes flight,
Stories born within the night.
Tranquil hearts will find their way,
Guided by the stars' ballet.

So let us bask in night's embrace,
Finding peace in time and space.
For within darkness, light will gleam,
Turning each shadow into a dream.

Garden of Ashes Under Starry Veil

In the garden where embers sleep,
The stars above begin to weep.
For every blossom born of pain,
A memory of love remains.

Beneath the velvety night sky,
Echoed whispers gently sigh.
The ashes scatter, dreams take wing,
Life regenerates, once more they sing.

Petals born from charred remains,
A tapestry of hopes and pains.
In the stillness, growth will rise,
Through the sorrow, beauty flies.

Timeless tales of loss and grace,
Each star holds a secret face.
Nurtured in the soil of strife,
A garden blooms, a brand new life.

Together, we shall tend this land,
With gentle hearts, and open hands.
Under starry veils, we will sow,
The seeds of love that always grow.

Lament of the Ash-Soaked Breeze

The breeze carries sorrow's song,
As whispers of ashes linger long.
Through the trees, a mournful plea,
Echoes softly, a memory free.

With every gust that sweeps the land,
A tale of loss, we understand.
In every curl of smoky air,
Lives a spirit, bold and rare.

The shadows dance, a fleeting sight,
Haunting dreams that fade from light.
Yet in the grief, a strength we find,
Unity effused through heart and mind.

Time shall weave its fabric tight,
Binding day to endless night.
And in each sigh of cooling air,
We feel the love that lingers there.

So let the ash-soaked breeze unite,
In remembrance of hearts that fight.
For in our cries, the world can see,
The beauty born from memory.

Breath of the Phoenix's Heart

In the depths of night, a flicker flies,
A dance of flames beneath the skies.
Resilient wings of crimson hue,
Reviving dreams that once rang true.

Echoed whispers from ages past,
Binding hearts in shadows cast.
Through valleys deep, in brilliance soar,
Awakening power, forevermore.

Ashes cradle hope's rebirth,
Embracing life, revealing worth.
A heartbeat echoes in the dark,
Igniting souls with a single spark.

Beneath the glow of an amber sun,
The phoenix rises—its journey begun.
It breathes the truth, it hums the grace,
In every dream, it finds its place.

With piercing cries that shatter doubt,
In gardens of fate, the heat breaks out.
Wings outspread, the future shines,
In the breath of hope, the heart defines.

Layers of Heat in the Quiet

When the world is hushed and dreams take flight,
The fire whispers, soft and bright.
Beneath the mantle of tranquil air,
Passions flicker, ignite with care.

Threads of warmth weave through the night,
Creating tapestries of gentle light.
Each secret spark, a story to tell,
In the silence, the flame casts its spell.

Soft embers dance in a lover’s gaze,
Igniting whispers in tender praise.
Hidden layers of warmth unfurl,
Creating magic in a bustling swirl.

Time suspends where the shadows lay,
And heat becomes the architect of day.
Through the quiet, passion flows,
In every ember, the heart knows.

In tender moments, let it be found,
The layers of heat, the solace profound.
As night fades into dawn's sweet light,
Awake, embrace the magic of night.

Reverence for the Forgotten Glow

In the echoes of time, a whisper remains,
A glow long faded, yet still sustains.
Through shadows deep, it still can be found,
A flicker of hope where silence is crowned.

Abandoned halls where dreams once dwelled,
In every corner, a story is held.
Memories dance in a ghostly embrace,
Yearning for warmth, for love, for grace.

With reverence, we gather the light,
Reviving remnants of radiant night.
In the dance of shadows, we see it rise,
A forgotten glow that never dies.

Let it remind us of paths once taken,
Of bonds unbroken, though time has shaken.
Through whispers of past, our hearts ignite,
In reverence bound, we embrace the light.

So here's to the glow, both tender and true,
In every heart, a warm hue.
For though it fades, it gracefully flows,
In the silence of love, the memory grows.

The Silence of Ancient Flames

Beneath the surface, the silence hums,
The heartbeat of fire as history comes.
Where shadows linger and secrets lie,
Ancient flames whisper; they never die.

In the quiet corners of forgotten lore,
Echoes of magic keep yearning for more.
Igniting with life, the embers awaken,
In silence profound, a promise is taken.

They flicker and fade, yet never depart,
Carving their presence in every heart.
Though time may dim their fiery breath,
The warmth persists, defying death.

Through soot and ash, the past survives,
In the silence of flames, the spirit thrives.
Stories emerge from the quiet gloom,
A dance of shadows, a vibrant bloom.

So let us listen to the ancient cries,
And honor the legacy that never dies.
For in silence profound, true wisdom remains,
A tapestry woven from ancient flames.

Embers in the Silence

In the quiet of the night, they gleam,
Flickering softly, like a stolen dream.
Whispers of warmth through shadows play,
Embers dance in a delicate sway.

Carried on breezes, secrets unfold,
Stories of fire, timeless and bold.
Silent guardians of the darkened glen,
Reminders of life, time and again.

Through the gloom, a soft sigh stirs,
A lingering hint of long-lost years.
Silent sparks speak of what once was,
In their glow, we find the cause.

Each flicker a tale, in silence spun,
Of battles lost, and victories won.
In every ember, a memory lies,
A testament to the passing skies.

Embers now fade, but hope reigns bright,
In the heart of darkness, a guiding light.
As long as we breathe, their presence stays,
In the whispers of night, we find our way.

Spirits of the Forgotten Sky

Beneath the vast and starry dome,
Spirits wander, far from home.
In the hush of night, they glide,
Over hills, where dreams reside.

Ethereal beings, lost to time,
In gentle currents, they intertwine.
With tales to tell of ancient strife,
They weave the fabric of our life.

Clouds of silver, shadows cast,
Echoes of futures, shadows of past.
Taking flight on whispered breeze,
They dance through the night with effortless ease.

In the stillness, their laughter rings,
Soft as the rustle of fluttering wings.
Elysium calls them home each night,
Yet they linger on, just out of sight.

Every star that twinkles high,
Is a memory of spirits nigh.
In their glow, we feel their grace,
A reminder of love’s warm embrace.

Whispers of Celestial Ash

In the depths of night, soft whispers fall,
Carried on winds, a muted call.
Celestial fragments from ages past,
Fleeting stories in shadows cast.

Ashes of dreams, scattered wide,
Telling tales of those who tried.
In every flicker, a life once known,
In the stillness, their seeds are sown.

Lunar beams cradle the serene,
Hushed confessions, delicate sheen.
Glimmers of hope in the dusky light,
A symphony woven, hidden from sight.

As the night unfolds its tender shroud,
Whispers rise, both soft and proud.
In the ashes, we find our spark,
Illuminating paths through the dark.

Each breath of night, rich with lore,
Inviting hearts to seek and explore.
Amidst the quiet, we hear their plea,
To hold their stories, wild and free.

Echoes in the Twilight Heat

As the sun dips low, shadows blend,
Echoes of twilight, messages send.
Whispers of warmth in the gathering haze,
Fleeting moments, a tender gaze.

Time slows within the dusky glow,
Secrets unravel, soft and slow.
A symphony rises in the crisp night air,
Unseen spirits weave without a care.

Beneath the blush of the closing day,
Echoes linger, then drift away.
In the heart of dusk, we breathe their song,
A melody echoed where dreams belong.

With every heartbeat, the twilight hums,
Nature's chorus, a rhythm that drums.
In the heat of the night, truths come alive,
In every whispered tale, we thrive.

Stars awaken, twinkling bright,
Guardians of hopes throughout the night.
In their light, echoes softly tread,
Tracing the paths where we dare to tread.

Serene Flames of Renewal

In the quiet woods where whispers play,
Gentle flames begin to sway,
A dance of light amidst the gloom,
Awakening life in the forest's womb.

Beneath the ashes, seeds lay tight,
Awaiting warmth, the dawn of light,
With each flicker, hope ignites,
Transforming shadows into sights.

The air is rich with earthy scents,
As nature's chorus transcends the vents,
From charred remains, new blooms arise,
Beneath the soft and azure skies.

Each spark a promise, pure and bright,
Whispering tales of endless night,
Yet kindling dreams of what will be,
In flames of gold, wild and free.

So let the world embrace the fire,
In its warmth, our hearts conspire,
For through the ashes, we shall see,
The serene flames of renewal, endlessly.

Dreams Drifting through Embered Skies

Beneath the twilight's gentle glow,
Dreams take flight on winds that flow,
Across the embers, softly gleam,
Rustling secrets, weaving dreams.

The stars above are like bright sparks,
Whispering wishes in the dark,
As shadows stretch and dance in sighs,
I chase my thoughts through embered skies.

A canvas painted with desire,
Colors blaze like tongues of fire,
Each heartbeat syncing with the night,
Guided by the soft, warm light.

With every flicker, visions rise,
In fleeting moments, hope defies,
The weight of doubt that tries to bind,
For in the dark, true paths we find.

So let me wander, let me soar,
With dreams that whisper, evermore,
Through embered skies, forever free,
Chasing the light of what could be.

Ghosts of Fire in the Stillness

In the silence, embers glow,
Whispers of warmth from long ago,
Ghostly figures dance and weave,
In the twilight, they deceive.

Fleeting shadows, soft and grand,
Trace the lines in sparkling sand,
Echoes of laughter, lost in time,
In this stillness, they do rhyme.

Red and gold, their colors fade,
Leaving behind the memories made,
In the night, their stories flow,
Carried forth by winds that know.

Though time may dim their flickered light,
Within the heart, they burn so bright,
A flame that warms the soul's deep core,
Ghosts of fire forevermore.

So listen close to the silent night,
Where spirits linger in pure delight,
For in the stillness, they softly plea,
To keep their glow, to set us free.

Muffled Cries of the Cinder Realm

In the depths where shadows creep,
Muffled cries begin to weep,
A realm of cinders, cold and bare,
Haunted whispers fill the air.

Flickering flames, a distant sound,
Echoes of life that's unbound,
In ashes deep, the truth does lie,
With every sigh, a heart's goodbye.

Yet through the gloom, a spark remains,
A flicker soft, breaking chains,
In muted tones, a plea for light,
To chase away the endless night.

With every ember, stories blend,
Softened voices of the friends,
Who once roamed wild, now lost in time,
In this cinder realm, they climb.

So let us heed their cautious calls,
In the silence where shadows fall,
For even in the darkest seam,
Hope rises high, a waking dream.

Silent Symphony of the Phoenix

In the quiet night where shadows blend,
A feathered echo whispers from the end.
With every rise, a tune of fate,
In silence, harmony shall await.

Through embers bright, lost hopes reclaim,
From ashes cold, a whispered name.
The melody soars on wings of fire,
Silent symphony, a heart's desire.

Beneath the stars where shadows grow,
The phoenix dances, fierce and slow.
Its song ignites the darkest skies,
A lullaby where magic lies.

With every note, the dawn shall break,
A world reborn, no heart to ache.
In twilight's hold, the whispers weave,
A silent promise, believe, believe.

So listen close, the night shall sing,
Of tales of hope that dawn will bring.
In this embrace, we all can find,
The silent symphony of the kind.

In the Wake of Wistful Flames

Upon the horizon, embers glow,
A dance of memories in the flow.
From flickering light, our stories rise,
In the wake of flames, dreams materialize.

Once lost to night, time flickers back,
In every spark, shadows shall not lack.
The warmth of past, forever we chase,
In wistful dreams, we find our place.

Whispers of hope in shadows blend,
Through fire's mystery, all will mend.
The heart's true hunger ignites our fates,
In the wake of flames, we open gates.

The crackling ashes, where secrets lay,
Hold tales untold of yesterday.
With every flicker, the past we trace,
In warmth and light, the world we embrace.

So linger near, as embers fade,
In the heart's glow, new paths are made.
From every flame, a legacy grows,
In the wake of time, our story flows.

Fable of the Ashen Sky

In twilight's hush, where shadows play,
The ashen sky begins to sway.
With tales of old, the stars align,
A fable spun transcending time.

Upon the wind, the echoes tell,
Of dreams long lost within their spell.
Each twinkling light, a story shared,
In ashen hues, we find what's spared.

With wings of night and whispers clear,
The fable calls to those who hear.
A journey waits in sapphire mist,
In the ashen sky, a heart's persist.

Through darkness thick, the truth shall shine,
A tapestry of the great design.
For in the void, we oft collide,
In every heart, the fable hides.

So raise your gaze to dreams of night,
In the ashen sky, there lies our light.
The fable whispers soft and slow,
A promise forged in stars aglow.

Ethereal Voices of Rejuvenation

In morning's light, the voices call,
With whispers sweet, they rise and fall.
A melody blooms, fresh as the dew,
Ethereal voices, forever true.

Through fields of green, the echoes play,
With every note, the world’s ballet.
In tender moments, life rekindles,
Ethereal songs where hope mingles.

As rivers flow, their secrets share,
A symphony woven in fragrant air.
In nature’s arms, we find our ground,
Ethereal voices, all around.

With every breath, new seasons greet,
In vibrant hues, our hearts repeat.
A tapestry of life's design,
Ethereal whispers, forever align.

So close your eyes and hear the song,
In nature’s breath, where we belong.
In every breeze, the past is spun,
Ethereal voices—life’s begun.

Reflections of a Soaring Spirit

In whispers soft, the winds do sing,
Of dreams unfurling on silvered wing.
Through valleys wide and mountains tall,
A spirit dances, heeds the call.

With each heartbeat, a tale will rise,
Beneath the vast and watchful skies.
Stars twinkle bright, a guiding map,
In night's embrace, I take a nap.

The echoes of laughter, of times gone by,
In every shadow, a spark will lie.
For every fall, a rise awaits,
With hope alight, a heart creates.

A tapestry woven from threads of gold,
In every story, the brave and bold.
Through all the trials that come and pass,
The spirit soars, like whispers in glass.

So let the journey lead me on,
To places where my heart belongs.
With each new dawn, I'll take my flight,
Reflections bright, in morning light.

Dimming Stars of a Fiery Past

Once fire blazed where shadows play,
Now embers dance, their glow does sway.
The tales of old hang heavy, tight,
As fading stars blink out of sight.

Memories flicker like fragile flames,
Whispers of laughter, forgotten names.
In a tapestry woven from dreams once spun,
The dusk descends, the day is done.

Yet even in dimness, hope does gleam,
In distant corners, a flickering dream.
With every heartbeat, I hold them dear,
The lessons learned, both far and near.

For time may dull the brightest glow,
But in the heart, the warmth will flow.
Each star that dims leaves space for new,
A fiery past can ignite the true.

So let the shadows weave their art,
In silence, they cradle the beating heart.
With every dawn, a promise made,
Dimming stars give way to the brighter cascade.

A Path Forged from the Ashen

From ashes cold, a journey starts,
Where hope is born in broken parts.
With every step, the ground does change,
The road ahead feels wide and strange.

Through whispered woods and mountains high,
I tread with care beneath the sky.
Each crack and crevice tells a tale,
Of dreams that soared, of hopes that pale.

The ghosts of yore resonate still,
In heartbeats matched, in muted thrill.
For every shadow, light will chase,
To forge a path, to find my place.

Through trials faced and battles won,
This road of ash has just begun.
With courage held, I'll rise, I'll climb,
For in the dark, I'll seek the rhyme.

So let this journey shape my soul,
In every step, I'll find my goal.
With every dawn, the path will bind,
A heart renewed, a spirit aligned.

Flight Stories of Dust and Light

In a world where dust and light collide,
The stories unfold on joy's swift ride.
Through every flurry, a tale is spun,
Of moonlit dreams and of the sun.

The gentle breeze carries whispers sweet,
Of secrets shared in soft retreat.
With every flutter, a memory wakes,
In the tapestry where magic breaks.

From the ground beneath, a lift takes flight,
Through shimmering veils of day and night.
Each grain of dust tells where we’ve been,
In landscapes vast, where we’ve seen.

So let the tales of wings take form,
In every heart, the fire will warm.
Through laughter bright and sorrows light,
We dance with shadows, embrace the night.

With every heartbeat, I weave my flight,
Through dust and light, in joy and plight.
In stories shared, I find my place,
In the dance of time, in the cosmic grace.

Embers Whisper Softly

In the hearth where shadows play,
Flickering flames ignite the night.
Echoes of warmth drift away,
Embers whisper, soft and bright.

Stories wrapped in smoky sighs,
Linger in the air so sweet.
Where love and loss gently ties,
In the stillness, hearts can meet.

Time slips through our grasp like sand,
But embers hold the dreams we save.
In the glow, we understand,
What memories the heart must brave.

Through the silence, sparks take flight,
Dancing on the edge of fate.
In the dark, a guiding light,
Embers whisper, never late.

So let the warmth embrace you still,
As shadows weave their tender dance.
In the quiet, find your will,
Embers whisper, take a chance.

Flight of the Shattered Echo

A silver bird on fractured wings,
Soars above the broken ground.
With every breath, the heart still sings,
Yet whispers of the lost resound.

Shattered dreams like glass take flight,
Crimson trails across the skies.
Each echo tells of faded light,
Memories woven in their cries.

In twilight's grasp, the shadows stir,
Carried on the winds of change.
Echoes call and softly purr,
In the silence, lives rearrange.

But with each tear the soul does shed,
A tapestry of strength is spun.
In every thread, a journey led,
A reminder that we're all one.

So when you feel you've lost your way,
Look skyward for the flight you seek.
For in the echoes, hope will stay,
To lift you when the heart feels weak.

Veils of Dusk and Dawn

In the land where shadows creep,
Veils of dusk, a soft embrace.
Whispers in the air, they seep,
Glimmers of a hidden grace.

As twilight drapes its cloak of blue,
Stars begin their nightly bloom.
In night's embrace, the world feels new,
While silence weaves a gentle loom.

Then, dawn arrives on tender feet,
Brushes skies in golden hues.
The harmonies of night retreat,
As light dispels the darkest views.

Each moment held, each breath anew,
In the dance of day and night.
Veils of dusk and dawn imbue,
The heart with hope, the soul with light.

So cherish every fleeting phase,
For beauty rests in change and flow.
In twilight's dream where shadows graze,
In dawn's warm grasp, our spirits grow.

Hush of the Charred Horizon

In the stillness of the night,
Where ashes dance in moonlight's gaze,
The horizon whispers, soft and tight,
A hush that cloaks the ashen blaze.

Winds carry tales of what's been lost,
Of battles fought and dreams once bright.
Yet through the pain, a gentle cost,
A promise blooms in the quiet light.

Through charred remains, new life will grow,
Beneath the weight of sorrow's past.
Each ember holds a story's glow,
Of how the fragile hearts hold fast.

As stars emerge from shadows deep,
Their shimmer echoes tales of yore.
In the hush where secrets sleep,
Hope takes root, forevermore.

So let the charred horizon speak,
Of journeys tough, yet souls refined.
In every hush, find strength to seek,
The beauty in what we leave behind.

Shadows Dancing Above the Hearth

In the flicker of ember's glow,
Shadows weave tales from long ago.
Whispers of secrets, soft and low,
Echoes of memories, a gentle flow.

Fireside tales of courage bright,
Dancing shadows in the night.
The warmth embraces, taking flight,
Weaving dreams, in flickering light.

Old stories linger, whispering near,
Of battles fought, of loves sincere.
Beneath the stars, no need to fear,
In this space, all hearts draw near.

Timeless moments, spun in gold,
The hearth's warm glow, a joy retold.
Through every flicker, warmth unfolds,
As shadows dance, their tales unfold.

So gather 'round, let your heart rest,
In the dance of shadows, feel the blessed.
For in this light, we are at our best,
In the hearth's embrace, we are caressed.

In the Afterglow of the Lost

When twilight whispers of the past,
In silence deep, we breathe, we last.
Memories linger, shadows cast,
In the afterglow, we hold them fast.

Beneath the stars, they softly gleam,
Of dreams once woven, like a dream.
In moonlit gardens, shadows scream,
Of fleeting moments, hearts that beam.

Echoes of laughter, bittersweet,
In phantom footsteps, we retreat.
The heart recalls a steady beat,
In the afterglow, we feel complete.

Yet in the stillness, we must learn,
To let the past fade, gently turn.
For life’s a light, a candle's burn,
In the afterglow, new dreams discern.

So send a message to the sky,
In the afterglow, we live, we fly.
For every lost, there's a new reply,
In the cycle of life, we learn to sigh.

Lullabies of the Smoldering Dawn

In the hush of dawn, dreams await,
Lullabies sung by the stars' fate.
With whispers soft, as shadows sate,
We find our path, embrace our state.

Through the fading night, light will creep,
Awakening thoughts from their deep sleep.
As heaven weaves its golden sweep,
In the smoldering dawn, our hearts leap.

With every breath, new hopes arise,
Beneath the veil of softening skies.
Each moment glimmers, brightly flies,
In lullabies sweet, the spirit ties.

Gather the dreams, hold them tight,
In the dawning glow, take your flight.
The world awakens, pure delight,
In the heart's embrace, endless night.

So sing along with the waking breeze,
For in the dawn, we find our keys.
In the smoldering light, let worries ease,
With lullabies whispered through the trees.

Resonance of the Reborn Flame

From ashes cold, the embers breathe,
In silence deep, rebirth we weave.
Through each flicker, we take leave,
Of shadows past, hopes that cleave.

The flame ignites with vibrant grace,
A dance of life in this sacred space.
It sings of love, of time's embrace,
Resonating in the heart's place.

Light spills forth, a bright cascade,
In every hue, dreams are made.
Through trials faced, we are remade,
In the reborn flame, fears do fade.

Hear the echoes of what's in store,
As the flames rise, they seek to soar.
In their warmth, we find the core,
Of life's great journey, evermore.

So embrace the light, let it remain,
For every heart holds love's refrain.
In the resonance of joy's sweet gain,
We rise anew, free from the chain.

When Hearts Take Wing

In twilight's gentle embrace, they soar,
With dreams unfurling, forever more.
Whispers of courage, soft and bright,
Guiding lost souls into the night.

A tapestry woven with strands of fate,
Each heart a traveler, none to wait.
Through laughter and tears, bonds intertwine,
In echoes of love, our spirits shine.

With wings of hope, we take to the skies,
Chasing the dawn, where freedom lies.
In every heartbeat, a story untold,
When hearts take wing, we're brave and bold.

Yet shadows may linger, doubts may arise,
But together we'll dance, beneath moonlit skies.
Unfurling our dreams like petals in spring,
In unity's strength, our spirits take wing.

And when the storms howl, and clouds grow dark,
We'll hold on to faith, ignite the spark.
For love is the compass that guides us through,
When hearts take wing, we'll find our true view.

Flickering Voices in the Air

In twilight's hush, a soft laugh floats,
Like fireflies dancing, on midnight's coats.
Flickering voices, they weave and sway,
Calling us gently, to where shadows play.

They whisper of secrets, both old and new,
Of dreams still lurking, in morning dew.
A symphony born from the breath of night,
Where shadows and starlight twine ever bright.

With each fleeting moment, the stories unfold,
Of brave-hearted wanderers, both young and old.
In each whispered tale, a spark ignites,
Flickering voices, like our hopes take flight.

The breeze carries murmurs of years long past,
Of trials faced bravely, of friendships cast.
We gather the fragments, hold them so near,
In flickering voices, our truths appear.

So listen, dear wanderer, to night's tender croon,
For in silent moments, our hearts find their tune.
Embrace every echo, each brilliance so rare,
In flickering voices, find magic to share.

Hiding in the Burnt Circles

Among the ashes, where embers glow,
Secrets lie hidden, the mind's shadow.
In burnt circles etched with tales of yore,
Hiding our whispers, forevermore.

Each mark a reminder of battles fought,
Of lessons learned and moments sought.
With wisdom as fire, we rise and fall,
In hiding, we learn to heed the call.

Through charred remains, new life may spring,
As hope and renewal take to the wing.
From the depths of sorrow, we gather our might,
Hiding in circles, we seek the light.

In every blaze, there's a spark of grace,
A path to redemption we must embrace.
Though shadows may linger, our spirits will soar,
Hiding in circles, we're forever more.

So let us rise up from the ashes deep,
Guided by dreams, awakened from sleep.
For in every ending, a new tale we weave,
Hiding in burnt circles, we believe.

Enigma of a Feathered Soul

In the heart of night, a raven calls,
Whispers of wisdom in shadowed halls.
A riddle unfolding, an ancient song,
The enigma of a soul, where all belong.

With feathers of starlight, it dances near,
Filling our minds with both hope and fear.
A journey of questions, where answers hide,
In search of the truth, we'll turn the tide.

Through forests of thought, we wander free,
In the hush of the twilight, we learn to see.
Each flutter a promise, a tale yet spun,
The enigma of a soul, where dreams are won.

In the tapestry woven from dusk till dawn,
We seek the connection, we ponder and yawn.
Yet in every heartbeat, the mystery grows,
Enigma of a feathered soul, it knows.

So chase the shadows and hug the light,
For woven together, wrong and right.
In the dance of creation, be brave and whole,
Embrace the enigma of your feathered soul.

Hushed Tales from the Ashen Heights

In the quiet of the night, whispers sound,
Old stories from the ashes, softly abound.
Beneath the stars, forgotten dreams do weave,
The secrets of the heights, the heart can believe.

Tales of flight on wings that spark with light,
Navigating shadows, a wondrous sight.
Where the echoes linger, wrapped in twilight's grace,
Ancient lore awakens in this sacred place.

Ashes tell of wonders lost to time's cruel hand,
Of a fire that danced, that once brightly spanned.
In the embers' glow, a magic reclaims,
The whispers of the past, calling out names.

Winds carry secrets, tales soar through the air,
With every flicker, we find we still care.
The ashen heights cradle both sorrow and glee,
In hushed, gentle tones, our hearts roam free.

So gather 'round the warmth, let the stories start,
For in every shadow, there beats a brave heart.
The tales of old flame, forever ignite,
In hushed tales from the ashen heights of night.

Flight of the Silent Rise

At dawn's first light, the silence takes flight,
On wings of twilight, they soar with delight.
Shadows stretch long, across the sky's hue,
A tranquil ascent, in a world anew.

From soft-spoken valleys, the whispers ascend,
To the heights of the heavens, where dreams apprehend.
Each heartbeat echoes in the morning's embrace,
As the silent rise unfolds in timeless grace.

Glimmers of hope dance in the chilly air,
Unraveled dreams float like feathers laid bare.
In the hush of the morn, as the light softly glows,
We find our resolve where the cool breeze flows.

With each lifted spirit, the burdens untwine,
In the silent rise, where the heart starts to shine.
No sound betrays the beauty of sights,
In this flight of the silent, all wrongs turn to rights.

So up we ascend, to the skies painted gold,
On wings of the silent, our stories unfold.
In the magic of morning, we rise and we soar,
In flight of the silent, we find evermore.

Ethereal Shades of Phoenix Light

From the ashes reborn, with colors ablaze,
The phoenix takes wing in a radiant haze.
Ethereal shades dance in the twilight's embrace,
Illuminating paths with elegance and grace.

Every feather aglow, a beacon of flame,
In the night sky glittering, no two are the same.
Whispers of magic weave through the night air,
In the glow of the phoenix, there's beauty to share.

Stories unfold in the flutter of wings,
Of strength in the struggle, of hope that clings.
Each rising moment, like soft morning light,
In ethereal hues, is a wondrous sight.

Together we dance with the shadows and bright,
Exploring the realms where the dreams take flight.
In each fleeting moment, a love takes its stand,
In ethereal shades, we are part of the grand.

So let your spirit soar with the flame’s fierce delight,
In the warmth of the dawn that follows the night.
For within every heart, the phoenix takes wing,
In ethereal shades, life’s praises we sing.

Murmurs from the Burnt Horizon

Beneath the burnt horizon, secrets reside,
In the shadows of silence, our dreams coincide.
Murmurs soft as whispers that dance on the crest,
Of hopes long forgotten, in time's gentle quest.

Flickers of warmth in the cool morning air,
Speak of journeys taken, of love laid bare.
As the shadows grow long, in the dusk's warm embrace,
We listen for echoes, of a lost time and place.

Every scar tells a story, in landscapes forlorn,
Where the cries of the heart, like old tales, are worn.
In the twilight's embrace, the horizon ignites,
With murmurs of courage that dazzle the nights.

Caught in the stillness, the world holds its breath,
As the remnants of fire resist the harsh death.
From the burnt horizon, the past starts to glow,
With murmurs of wisdom, only shadows can know.

So gather the tales of the brave and the bold,
In whispers of night, let your spirit unfold.
For from the burnt horizon, new journeys begin,
In the heart of the dusk, we breathe deep within.

Preserved Whispers of Rebirth

In ancient woods where shadows sleep,
The secrets stir, the roots grow deep.
Each whispered tale, a tale reborn,
In twilight's breath, a world is worn.

The tender buds break through the frost,
In fragile light, the past is lost.
From dust to bloom, the cycle calls,
In every rise, a memory falls.

With every reaping of the sky,
A hopeful heart begins to fly.
Through gentle rains and sunny beams,
We find the light within our dreams.

The echoes linger, soft yet strong,
In whispered hymns, a timeless song.
They speak of change, of love and pain,
Of every joy that springs from rain.

In twilight's glow, the stories weave,
A tapestry that bids us believe.
For in their threads, we find our part,
A map of life, a work of art.

Serenity Amongst the Cinders

In the silence where embers glow,
A hush descends, the breezes flow.
With every spark that fades away,
A memory of night turns day.

Amongst the ashes, a life remains,
The whispers of past, the soft refrains.
From heart of fire, calm descends,
In solitude, the spirit mends.

The shadows dance with dusky grace,
While peace wraps 'round like a warm embrace.
Each flicker holds a secret swayed,
In cinders' glow, our fears are laid.

As twilight descends, the stars ignite,
In cosmic eyes, our hopes take flight.
With every dream that starts to glide,
Serenity is ours to bide.

The quiet ember, the soothing balm,
In gentle breaths, we find our calm.
So let the night embrace the fire,
In cinders' warmth, we never tire.

The Softening Touch of Fire

The fire flickers, shadows play,
In molten hues, the night gives way.
With every crackle, warmth ignites,
Wrapped in glow, our souls take flight.

Beneath this ember's tender hum,
A heartbeat whispers, soft and numb.
Through flames that dance with wild delight,
We find our truth, our dark, our light.

The tongue of flame, a gentle friend,
In its embrace, all sorrows mend.
With each soft flick, the past takes flight,
Thus life unfurls, a tapestry bright.

As moments shift with amber's grace,
The fiery touch, a warm embrace.
In every spark, a story sings,
Of hopes anew and fragile things.

In midnight's glow, we find our way,
The fire's soft touch, our guiding ray.
So let it burn, let shadows fade,
In every light, again remade.

A Landscape of Shattered Dreams

In fields where whispers lost their way,
The echoes linger, soft yet gray.
With every step, the shadows loom,
A landscape weeps, a heart in gloom.

The fragments glisten, sharp and bright,
Each shard a memory of lost flight.
In every tear, a tale remains,
Of hopes that danced in silver rains.

Amongst the ruins, flowers bloom,
In gentle grace, they pierce the gloom.
Resilience found in fractured light,
A tapestry of day and night.

Yet in this place where dreams have bled,
The spirit rises, not yet dead.
From ashes cold, a fire can grow,
In shattered landscapes, beauty flows.

So let us walk through broken lands,
Embracing hope with open hands.
For in the cracks, the light will gleam,
And from the dust, we'll weave our dream.

Beneath A Canopy of Loss

Beneath a sky, so dark and wide,
Memories linger, they cannot hide.
Whispers of the past, they call,
Echoing softly, through it all.

Leaves that rustle, secrets kept,
Where shadows roam, and silence wept.
In the heart's garden, once so bright,
Now blooms the sorrow, void of light.

But strength is found in the bleakest night,
As stars emerge, with hope's soft light.
Each tear that falls, a river flows,
Nurturing growth, where no one knows.

Time weaves ribbons, of grief and grace,
In the tapestry of a haunting place.
Yet love transforms, the pain we bear,
A tribute to those, forever there.

So let us wander, hand in hand,
Through the thickets of this barren land.
For beneath the canopy, where shadows play,
Lies the promise of dawn, a brand new day.

Glowing Reflections of the Soul

In a still pond, where dreams take flight,
Ripples dance, in the soft twilight.
Voices echo, secrets unfold,
In glowing reflections, stories told.

Every shimmer, a distant star,
Guiding lost hearts, from near and far.
Each shadow twirls, a fleeting form,
In the twilight's embrace, so warm.

Thoughts like feathers, light and free,
Carried softly, on the breeze.
Whispers of laughter, bittersweet toy,
In the depths of the heart, lies joy.

Through the mirrors of our eye,
We glimpse the truth, and learn to fly.
Let the soul shine, through darkest seams,
For within us all, live bright dreams.

Time is fleeting, yet moments last,
In glowing reflections, we hold fast.
With every ripple, we see it clear,
The dance of life, unbound and dear.

The Stillness After the Flame

After the fire, where embers sigh,
Amidst the ashes, dreams still lie.
A hush falls gently, the world held breath,
In the quietude, we dance with death.

The warmth of glow, now but a trace,
Memories linger, in their embrace.
Through the desolation, new life may sprout,
From the stillness, we learn to shout.

Whispers of hope, in weary hearts,
From the silence, a new beating starts.
In every ending, a beginning waits,
A chance for growth, as fate dictates.

The night's despair, it softly fades,
In the dawn’s light, new courage raids.
What once was lost in the searing pain,
Now blooms with promise, life’s sweet gain.

So let the ashes, remind and bind,
The strength we gather, the love we find.
For after the flame, the stillness so sweet,
Is where we gather, and life’s pulse beats.

Harmonies Born from Embers

In the cool dusk, where shadows blend,
Harmonies rise, and sorrows mend.
Embers crackle, a spirit's song,
In the heart's echoes, we belong.

The warmth of voices, intertwined,
Playing melodies, gentle, kind.
With every note, the soul takes flight,
Dancing within, the stars ignite.

Time holds stories, as old as night,
In every silence, a hidden light.
From the ashes, we find our way,
Creating harmonies, day by day.

Each breath is music, sweet and deep,
In the lullabies, our dreams we keep.
Let go of shadows, embrace the glow,
For within the embers, love will grow.

Together we rise, from the darkened place,
With harmonies born, of hope and grace.
From the depths of heartache, let voices soar,
Through the music of life, forevermore.

Solitude in the Rising Smoke

In the hush of dawn's embrace,
Thoughts drift like wisps of mist,
Chasing shadows, lost in grace,
Where silence holds what skies have kissed.

Faint echoes call from distant lands,
While the sun peeks through the grey,
A dance of dreams in failing hands,
As night surrenders to the day.

Embers whisper tales untold,
Of journeys taken, hearts set free,
Of warmth in the dark, within the cold,
In solitude's arms, a mystery.

With every breath, the smoke will curl,
Each swirl a memory, bittersweet,
Of a world spun into a whirl,
A tapestry both fragile and discrete.

Yet in this calm, a secret grows,
A spark ignites beneath the gloom,
For in stillness, strength bestows,
Life's promise flowers amidst the doom.

Tapers of Light Amidst the Ash

Flickering candles, spirits rise,
Through smoke, they weave an ancient song,
Softly glimmering, like stars in skies,
Amidst the ash, where dreams belong.

Each tapers' glow, a sacred spark,
Guiding us through the darkest nights,
In the quietness, where shadows embark,
Whispers of hope in fragile lights.

Journeys borne on wings of flame,
Threads of courage, woven fast,
Through the embers, we stake our claim,
An echo of futures, unsurpassed.

For ashes cradle wisdom's warmth,
In each flicker, the past shall guide,
Through darkest times, a steadfast charm,
Under the watchful, glowing tide.

So let the tapers brightly shine,
Illuminating paths once lost,
In every heart, a light divine,
To rise above the bitter frost.

Murmurs of Flight in Still Air

In tranquil moments, whispers rise,
Where stillness wraps the earth in peace,
A flutter soft beneath the skies,
Tales of flight that never cease.

Wings unfurl in silent grace,
Dancing lightly on the breeze,
Each beat, a heartbeat, time and space,
Entwined in wonders that never tease.

The world below, a canvas wide,
Colors blending, shades of dreams,
In the solitude of sky's pride,
Life's magic flows in endless streams.

In every murmur, secrets trace,
Of journeys yet to be unfurled,
As shadows play in lighted space,
In still air, a quest for the world.

So let us listen, hearts awake,
To murmurs soft that call us near,
In the silence, let courage stake,
A claim on dreams we hold so dear.

Shadowsong of Rising Wings

Beneath the moon's soft silver gaze,
Shadows dance upon the ground,
A song of wings in twilight's haze,
Whispered secrets, softly found.

In every rustle, stories weave,
Of freedom on the winds that soar,
A tapestry of dreams that cleave,
To hearts that wander evermore.

Each feather falls, a silent plea,
To rise above the earthly ties,
In shadowsong, we can be free,
Embracing life where spirit flies.

Through darkened paths, the light will break,
Guiding souls who dare to climb,
For in this dance, all fears will shake,
And rise on wings, escaping time.

So heed the call, the night shall sing,
Of journeys bold that lie ahead,
In shadows soft, where courage springs,
We find our strength, our spirits fed.

Shadows on a Fading Ember

In twilight whispers, shadows creep,
They dance with secrets, wild and deep.
Each ember fades, a flickering light,
Casting dreams into the night.

Ancient tales in solemn air,
Echo softly, a gentle prayer.
Beneath the stars, the heart does yearn,
For lost adventures, we may learn.

The moonlight bathes the quiet trees,
While ghosts of laughter ride the breeze.
Time drips slowly, a golden stream,
We chase the shadows of our dream.

Yet in the dark, new hope can shine,
For every ember, there's a sign.
With every breath, we take a chance,
To weave our fates in this old dance.

So gather round the dying spark,
Let stories linger in this dark.
For even as the embers fade,
The tales we share will never jade.

Legends in the Emptied Skies

Above the world, the legends soar,
In emptied skies forevermore.
The stars are whispers, soft and bright,
Guiding lost souls through the night.

They speak of warriors, brave and bold,
Of realms of magic, tales of old.
When shadows stretch across the land,
These echoes still, like grains of sand.

In every breeze, a story swells,
In whispered tones, the magic dwells.
The constellations weave their lore,
In moonlit dreams, forevermore.

So lift your gaze when darkness falls,
And hear the voice of ancient calls.
For in the heavens, bright and wide,
Legends dance, and hopes abide.

We are but wanderers in time,
Searching for the perfect rhyme.
With every heartbeat, love persists,
In emptied skies, our dreams exist.

Glistening Halo of Silence

In the stillness, a halo gleams,
With whispers caught in silver dreams.
The world hushes, breath held tight,
As shadows play in gentle light.

A tranquil spell, the silence flows,
Where hope and wonder softly grows.
Each moment wrapped in fragile grace,
In quietude, we find our place.

The stars watch over, serene and bright,
Guardians of the vast, deep night.
As dawn approaches, the stillness sighs,
In glistening halos, love never dies.

With every heartbeat, peace unfolds,
Stories waiting, yet untold.
In silence, dreams take flight and soar,
Emboldened souls, forevermore.

In the calm, we seek our truth,
A sliver of hope, a hint of youth.
For in the stillness, dreams awaken,
In glistening halos, hearts unshaken.

Fractured Flames of Remembrance

Within the dark, a flicker glows,
A fractured flame, where memory flows.
It dances gently, casting shade,
Of laughter lost, and love displayed.

Each spark a story, once so bright,
Now dimmed by shadows, veiled in night.
Yet in their glow, we find the past,
A bittersweet bond that holds us fast.

In whispered echoes, the flames confide,
Of battles fought and dreams denied.
They flicker low, yet still, they yearn,
For all the lessons we can learn.

Through smoldering ash, the heart can see,
The beauty forged in memory.
In every crack, a tale remains,
Of fractured flames that spark again.

So gather close, and share the light,
Transform the dark, embrace the night.
For though the flames may fade away,
The flames of love will always stay.

Celestial Dance of the Reborn

Stars awaken in velvet skies,
Soft whispers cradle night's sighs.
Galaxies twirl in ageless grace,
Spirits return to a new embrace.

Winds of change weave through the trees,
Echoes of laughter drift on the breeze.
From shadows deep, hope takes its stand,
Light spilling forth from a guiding hand.

Mists of dreams begin to swirl,
In cosmic realms, tales unfurl.
Flickers of life in twilight's glow,
Dance with the moon, a celestial show.

The sky ignites with colors bright,
Every heartbeat, a spark of light.
In this vast expanse of time,
The reborn sing in perfect rhyme.

As dawn approaches, they intertwine,
With the sun's warmth, a love divine.
With each moment, they take their flight,
In the celestial dance of endless night.

The Calm of the Forgotten Fire

In the silence where embers lay,
Whispers of warmth refuse to stray.
A once-bright flame now flickers low,
Yet in its glow, memories flow.

Threads of gold in the ashes found,
Stories linger, mute but profound.
Cool shadows wrap the hearth's embrace,
Whilst dreams still dance in a timeless space.

The night is deep; the world stands still,
Reflecting on the fire's thrill.
Comfort rests in the quiet air,
A gentle heart that knows to care.

Moments cherished, though time has passed,
A flicker amidst shadows cast.
In the calm that takes the night,
The forgotten fire burns softly bright.

When dawn arrives, its glow will find,
The warmth revived, the ties redefined.
In every heart, a spark's desire,
To rekindle what the years retire.

A Symphony of Ash and Light

From the ashes, a melody plays,
Notes of hope in the softest rays.
In the quiet where embers sing,
Lies the beauty that new dawns bring.

The world transforms with each refrain,
Harmony dances through each pain.
In shadows where loss leaves its mark,
A chorus swells, igniting the spark.

Brighter than sun on a summer's eve,
In every heartbeat, we dare believe.
The past embraced, yet gently released,
A symphony rich in love's feast.

Fire and ash, a tender theme,
Within the dark, we find the dream.
Each note a thread, weaving in flight,
A tapestry woven of ash and light.

From chaos born, a song will rise,
Uniting lost souls beneath the skies.
In the end, with feelings so bright,
We find our peace in the dance of light.

Lull in the Heart of the Hearth

In the heart of the home, a warm glow glimmers,
The hearth cradles dreams, as sweet hope simmers.
Soft blankets of night fall gently near,
While whispers of love wrap us dear.

Fires flicker with tales long spun,
Of laughter shared and battles won.
In forgotten corners, memories hide,
And within these walls, we abide.

Every crackle holds a story old,
A symphony of warmth that never grows cold.
The heartbeat of this space, it sings,
Of comfort found in simple things.

So gather close as the twilight dims,
Let the light guide where each heart swims.
In this lull, we're free from strife,
The hearth's embrace, the dance of life.

As shadows play in waltzing grace,
We find our place in this timeless space.
With every breath, we feel it start,
The lull in the soul, a lull in the heart.

Subtle Murmurs of Ash

In shadows where the embers fade,
Whispers linger, soft yet staid.
The smoke curls up, a tale untold,
Of dreams once bright, now silent gold.

With every breath, the past awakes,
In fragile forms, the memory shakes.
A flicker here, a sigh from yore,
The heart remembers, longs for more.

As time weaves through the dusky air,
Echoes dance, a ghostly pair.
From ashes rise a quiet grace,
In twilight's hold, we find our place.

The night enfolds, a velvet hue,
In softer tones, the world feels new.
In hallowed silence, peace bestows,
The subtle murmur of what goes.

So heed the Ash, both fierce and kind,
For in its song, our ties unwind.
A gentle pulse beneath the crust,
In every pulse, there lies the dust.

Twilight's Hidden Serenade

When day dips low and stars ignite,
The world hums soft, a cloak of night.
In hidden groves, the shadows play,
A serenade, where secrets lay.

Whispers weave through twilight’s seam,
Entwined in nature’s gentle dream.
The moon, a guide, with silvery glance,
Invites the heart to dare a dance.

With every note, the spirits soar,
In rustling leaves, they sing of lore.
A symphony of quiet grace,
In every whisper, we find a place.

As crickets chirp in rhythmic glee,
The night unfolds its mystery.
The world retreats, yet we remain,
In twilight’s arms, a sweet refrain.

So let us linger, lost in tune,
Beneath the watchful eyes of moon.
For in this hour, magic gleans,
In twilight’s heart, our spirit dreams.

Resurgence in the Stillness

In the calm where shadows dwell,
Quiet whispers softly swell.
In stillness blooms a tender grace,
Paths of time we gently trace.

With every pause, the world transforms,
In silence, beauty brightly warms.
A heartbeat echoes, faint yet clear,
A call to rise, to persevere.

Through fragile moments, strength will bloom,
From quiet corners, dispel the gloom.
In starlit voids, the dreams ignite,
With every breath, we spark the light.

Resurgence born of thoughtful breath,
In stillness whispers life from death.
The heart renews, the spirit flies,
In sacred hush, our courage lies.

So let the quiet guide our way,
In stillness find what words don't say.
For in the calm, we learn to rise,
In tender strength, the spirit sighs.

Echoes of a Phoenix Rise

From the ashes, embers gleam,
A flicker shines, a whispered dream.
In fiery gold, the phoenix soars,
Defying fate, it boldly roars.

The flames of loss, they feed the fire,
In every scar, a heart's desire.
With wings outstretched, the past is shed,
In bursts of light, the soul is led.

From darkest night to morning's grace,
The phoenix claims its rightful place.
In vibrant hues, the world reborn,
From every ending, hope is sworn.

So rise again, let spirits thrive,
From embers lost, we all survive.
In each rebirth, we learn to rise,
Through echoes soft, the phoenix flies.

The dance of flames, a fierce embrace,
In swirling heat, our fears displaced.
With every rise, our voices blend,
In echoes bold, we find our end.

www.ingramcontent.com/pod-product-compliance
Ingram Content Group UK Ltd.
Pitfield, Milton Keynes, MK11 3LW, UK
UKHW051100290125
4330UKWH00065B/484